Understanding Solid State Drives
The Future of Storage

Table of Contents

Chapter 1. Introduction

Demystifying the technological advancements of storage capabilities, our Special Report, "Understanding Solid State Drives: The Future of Storage," breaks down the complex landscape of data storage in a palatable and user-friendly manner. Without delving too far into the nitty-gritty, we provide an insightful look at how the poised emergence of Solid State Drives (SSDs) revolutionizes our interaction with technology. This report pins down the rudiments of SSDs, the advantages they offer over traditional storage devices, and previews the promising future they hold - all in a simplified, engaging format. Whether you're a tech enthusiast or a casual user looking to upgrade their technological know-how, this modish unveiling of the future of storage is tailored just for you. So come, join us on this enlightening journey as we explore the imminent frontier of data storage.

Chapter 2. The Emergence of Solid State Drives

It's crucial to remember the profound influence of Moore's Law: a prediction made by Gordon Moore in 1965 that the number of transistors in a dense integrated circuit will double approximately every two years. This law has held remarkably true for semiconductor technologies, including the Solid State Drives that we will now discuss.

2.1. A Break from Tradition: Evolution of Storage Devices

The journey of data storage, from punch cards in the early 19th century to the cloud storage of the modern era, is truly fascinating. Traditional magnetic storage, or hard disk drives (HDDs), have been the stalwarts of storage for decades. From running operating systems to storing movies, HDDs have underpinned the rise of the Information Age. However, the challenges faced by HDDs - such as slower read-write speeds, vulnerability to physical shock, heat generation, and larger power consumption - have paved the way for the emergence of Solid State Drives (SSDs).

SSDs brought the much-needed breath of fresh air in the technology world. These drives, known for their speed, durability, energy efficiency, and quiet operation, use no moving parts, and store information on microchips, much like your computer's temporary memory (RAM), but with the capability of retaining the data even when powered off.

2.2. Unpacking the Architecture of SSDs

The core components of an SSD include a controller, a connector, NAND flash memory chips, and a capacitor. Let's get into the functioning of each:

1. Flash Controller: This unit manages the data stored on an SSD. It handles tasks such as error checking, data distribution, and connecting the drive to the rest of the computer system via the interface.

2. NAND Flash Memory Chips: The chips store data within the drive. Unlike HDDs, the data in NAND chips can be accessed directly, which significantly improves speed. It also ensures data retention even when the drive is not powered.

3. Capacitor: The capacitor provides power to the drive in case of sudden power supply interruption, mitigating the chances of data corruption.

4. Connector: The connector links the SSD to the rest of the computer system through interfaces such as SATA, PCIe, or NVMe.

2.3. Advantages of SSDs over Traditional HDDs

Solid State Drives offer numerous benefits over their HDD counterparts:

1. Speed: SSDs outclass HDDs in terms of speed, performing up to ten times faster in read/write operations. This speed not only facilitates faster system boots and shorter application load times, but it also improves the overall system responsiveness.

2. Durability: Because SSDs employ NAND flash memory and do not

possess any moving parts, they are less prone to physical shock, making them far more durable and reliable than HDDs.

3. Energy Efficiency: SSDs require less power to operate than HDDs, resulting in longer battery life for portable devices like laptops and tablets.

4. Silent Operation: SSDs produce no mechanical noise, offering a quieter working environment.

2.4. The Changing Landscape of Data Storage and Emerging Trends

The ubiquitous computing devices we utilise every day produce colossal amounts of data. In the age of big data and machine learning, these data need to be stored, accessed, and processed quickly and efficiently. SSDs are rising to the occasion, revolutionising the storage industry.

Crucial trends are reshaping the landscape of this technology:

1. NVMe Over Fabrics (NVMe-oF): This revolutionary technology allows SSDs to perform at their peak even over a network by significantly reducing latency.

2. QLC NAND: Quad Level Cell (QLC) is the latest advancement in flash memory, which increases the storage capacity of individual flash cells, enabling SSDs to achieve larger capacities at a lower cost.

3. AI and Machine Learning: As AI and machine learning applications proliferate, they generate considerable data that requires rapid processing. SSDs, with their high speed and energy efficiency, are well-suited to meet these challenges.

2.5. The Forward Leap: What's Next in SSD Technology?

SSDs are not static technology. Manufacturers continually innovate to overcome the limitations of the current generation of SSDs. One such innovation that is taking the world of storage by storm is Optane technology by Intel. Optane SSDs are based on Intel's 3D XPoint memory technology, which is faster, denser, and more durable than NAND flash memory.

Another promising future technology is NVMe 2.0, the 'next big thing' in SSD interfaces. It is designed to make SSDs more efficient and even faster than they are now. Further, SSD manufacturers are also working on Multi-Actuator technology. It essentially aims to read and write data from two parts of an SSD simultaneously, thereby doubling its performance.

As we venture into the uncharted territories of quantum computing and DNA storage, the potential of SSDs only becomes increasingly intriguing. It is clear that SSDs, with their fast-paced evolution and agility to adapt to new technological landscapes, are here to stay and conquer the future of data storage.

As the contours of data storage continue to shift, riding the wave of SSDs is no longer a choice but a necessity for businesses and individuals. Staying informed and adapting to these shifts can truly unlock unprecedented levels of performance and efficiency. Buckle up and prepare yourself to witness an exciting future of data storage, powered by Solid State Drives.

Chapter 3. From Hard Disk Drives to Solid State Drives: A Transformation

Voyaging through the annals of digital data storage, our path crosses different types of technologies. From punch cards and magnetic tapes to floppy discs and compact discs, a myriad variety of storage mediums have been developed over time. Two primary contenders that dominated a substantial part of this journey are Hard Disk Drives (HDDs) and, more recently, Solid State Drives (SSDs).

3.1. The Analogous Journey of HDDs

Since the advent of digital storage, HDDs have primarily been the go-to storage medium. A hard disk drive is an electromechanical device with an actuator arm that lays data onto the storage medium or retrieves it. On a microscopic level, a hard drive works similarly to a record player. A series of disks coated in magnetic material spins at a phenomenal speed, while the actuator arm reads or writes data onto these disks, the platters, creating an array of 0s and 1s - the binary language computers comprehend.

HDDs gained favor due to the balance they struck between cost, data capacity, and speed. Their sequential data read-write prowess made them the de facto choice for general computing needs and, to date, establish their presence in many a storage solution.

However, HDDs have also seen their share of challenges - substantial power consumption, noticeable noise during operation, degradation over the years, susceptibility to physical factors like jolts or magnetic exposure, and relatively slow data access times. As technology evolved, seeking enhanced speed and energy efficiency became inevitable, paving the way for the emergence of SSDs.

3.2. Emergence of Solid State Drives

Enter the Solid State Drive - a storage device that touts superior performance, efficiency, and reliability, marching a step closer to the desired future of storage solutions.

SSDs make use of flash memory to store data rather than the rotating platters used in HDDs. Flash memory is a type of non-volatile memory that can be electronically erased and reprogrammed. It's called 'solid-state' because it has no moving mechanical parts. This unique attribute makes SSDs faster, quieter, and more robust - they're less likely to fail due to physical shocks, unlike HDDs.

SSDs function on the principles of electron tunneling, essentially controlling the flow of electrons across a barrier in a semiconductor, leading to data being stored or erased.

3.3. The Comparative Advantage: SSDs vs HDDs

The intrinsic technological advantage of using SSDs over HDDs marks a critical turning point in the way we store data.

Speed is one of the most compelling comparative advantages. Unlike HDDs, SSDs don't have a moving read/write head, which means they don't need to sequentially read data. Consequently, random read-write speeds are significantly faster with SSDs, leading to nearly instantaneous data access, faster boot times, rapid file transfers, and brisk application launches.

In addition to speed, SSDs have several other advantages over HDDs. They're remarkably energy-efficient, consuming a fraction of the power an HDD does. They make almost no noise, they're far less prone to mechanical failure, and they function unaffected by magnetism, a significant HDD weak point.

From a physical size perspective as well, SSDs are more compact, representing a substantial space economy, particularly important in mobile devices and laptops.

However, it's worth noting that SSDs aren't devoid of disadvantages. For instance, SSDs are costlier per gigabyte than HDDs. Also, while SSDs are more robust when it comes to general wear and tear, they have finite read-write cycles, after which the cells become unusable. Still, under most usage conditions, an SSD will likely last longer than the device it's powering.

3.4. The Transformation Towards SSDs: Unprecedented and Promising

The march from HDDs to SSDs represents more than just a technological shift; it depicts an evolution in our understanding and utilization of digital data storage. SSDs not only drastically cut down on mechanical limitations inherent to traditional storage devices but offer performance outputs far superior.

Today, with SSDs aiding processes from everyday computing functions to running high-end servers and data centers, our reliance on these incredible devices is growing. Commercial SSDs developments have surged in capacity and plummeted in cost, making them increasingly more available and affordable to consumers. Concurrent technological advancements continue to push SSDs' capabilities, such as 3D NAND technology that vertically stacks memory cells, dramatically increasing storage capacity and lowering production costs.

Despite their relatively high cost per gigabyte, SSDs' multitude of advantages makes them a promising player in the future of digital storage, potentially phasing out HDDs in many applications.

In summary, our journey of transformation from HDDs to SSDs has been a captivating one, underlined by technological innovation and evolution. As we forge ahead, we anticipate that SSDs, with their expanding possibilities and continuous advancements, will continue to revolutionize data storage. In this ever-evolving sphere of digital technology, the promising potentials of SSDs mark an exciting era ahead.

Chapter 4. Components and Inner Workings of SSDs

Before embarking on our exploration of the inner workings of Solid State Drives (SSDs), it's pertinent to understand the format of these devices. SSDs herald a paradigm shift from the traditional data storage - obsolete Hard Disk Drives (HDDs) - by employing a type of flash memory known as NAND.

Though the basic function of storage is preserved, SSDs are a wholly different creature under the hood, housing several components which work together harmoniously to provide speedy, efficient data storage and access.

4.1. The NAND Flash Memory

At the heart of the SSD, holding the core function, is the NAND flash memory. This non-volatile form of memory - meaning it doesn't require continuous power to retain stored information - is the primary storage medium in an SSD, built to hold data even when the system is switched off or encounters sudden power loss.

NAND flash memory is made up of numerous cells, which store bits of data. Depending on the type of NAND memory (SLC, MLC, TLC, QLC), these cells can store between one to four bits each. Each cell's state can be changed or handled individually, providing SSDs a significant edge over HDDs.

4.2. SSD Controller

The SSD controller is the brains behind the operation. This component is responsible for communicating between the SSD storage and the computer's system. It handles tasks like error correction, wear leveling, bad block mapping, and encryption; all of these contribute to the health and longevity of the SSD.

When data is written to the SSD, the controller decides where each piece goes, while also managing the demands of the host system. The quality and capability of the SSD controller can dramatically influence the drive's overall performance and reliability.

In essence, the controller's primary purpose is to ensure the NAND Flash Memory is operating as efficiently as possible.

4.3. Wear Leveling

Wear leveling is a process managed by the SSD controller to evenly distribute writes across the SSD's storage. This distribution is crucial because each cell within an SSD has a limited number of write cycles before it starts to fail. By spreading out the writes, the SSD can maximize its lifespan, a process called wear leveling.

SSDs typically use one of two types of wear leveling: static and dynamic. Dynamic wear leveling directs new data to the least used cells, while static wear leveling does the same but also ensures data stored long-term is moved, so all cells wear evenly.

4.4. Over-Provisioning

Over-provisioning refers to a storage space set aside in the SSD that isn't available to users but is available to the SSD controller. A higher level of over-provisioned space often results in improved SSD performance because the controller can use this space to better manage data placement, wear leveling, and background activities.

This whole scheme works together to sustain the SSD's speedy operations and longevity.

4.5. DRAM Cache

Many SSDs contain a DRAM component, a type of volatile memory that provides temporary workspace for the SSD controller. SSDs utilize the DRAM cache for their mapping tables. These tables hold the physical location of data blocks, and by storing these in quick-access DRAM rather than slower NAND cells, the SSD's speed and efficiency can be dramatically increased.

However, because DRAM requires power to retain information, loss of power means losing data in the DRAM cache. Modern SSDs, though, implement power-loss protection methods like capacitors to guard against such data loss.

4.6. Bad Block Management

During the lifespan of the SSD, some cells may become faulty - these are labeled 'bad blocks'. Efficiently managing and avoiding these bad blocks is key to the overall SSD performance. The wear-leveling process, under the control of the controller, is involved in this operation.

The controller keeps track of bad blocks and avoids writing new data to these areas. Instead, it re-routes this data to good cells, preserving the integrity of the stored data and the health of the SSD.

From the NAND flash memory to the sophisticated SSD controller, each component of the SSD has its unique role to play. Beyond the assembly and functions of these components, SSDs incorporate advanced processes and techniques like wear leveling, over-provisioning, and bad block management to ensure optimal performance, speed, and lifespan. As our dependence on data expands, so too does the complexity and capability of the devices that store it.

Chapter 5. Benefits of Solid State Drives: Speed and Durability

Emergence of Solid State Drives (SSDs) has ushered in an era where speed and durability have become paramount features in the paradigm of data storage. SSDs, with their unique structural design, lack of moving parts, and cutting-edge memory technology, have challenged the common notion of traditional storage devices, and are redefining the future of storage.

5.1. Speed: A Game Changer

Speed stands as a critical factor for determining performance in computing. From load times to file transfers, the speed at which data can be accessed has considerable influences on overall system performance. SSDs have shown major advancements in this field over traditional Hard Disk Drives (HDDs).

In SSDs, data is stored in NAND flash memory, which does not rely on any physical read/write head. The absence of moving parts enables an SSD to access stored data swiftly, providing read and write speeds that vastly exceed those of HDDs. An average SSD can operate at speeds of around 550 megabytes per second (MB/s) for reads and 520 MB/s for writes, as opposed to HDDs which typically operate at a rate of only 125 MB/s. This significant increase in speed results in a noticeable improvement in the system's performance.

Also, it's worth noting, SSDs suffer none of the fragmentation issues that can slow HDDs down, as data can be read from any location without any additional delay.

5.1.1. Speed Benefits in Everyday Computing

The high speeds that SSDs boast of, bring along considerable impacts in everyday computing tasks. A computer with an SSD boots significantly faster, and applications launch promptly without setting users on a waiting spree. This rapidity also translates positively when dealing with data-intensive tasks such as large file transfers, rendering videos or running high-end games. Truly, speed forms the lynchpin of the sort of enhanced user experience that SSDs bring.

5.1.2. Speed Benefits in Professional Settings

In professional environments catering to data-intensive work, such as data centers, animation studios or financial trade floors, the high-speed performance of SSDs proves to be a befitting choice. Their ability to handle large amounts of data rapidly, significantly reduces system lag and latency. This enables companies to improve their productivity, deliver services faster, and maintain a competitive edge in their respective fields.

5.2. Durability: Redefining Lifespan

The relative durability of SSDs compared to HDDs is another pivotal feature that makes them a compelling choice. The superior durability of SSDs can be attributed to the absence of moving parts in their structure, making them less susceptible to physical damage.

HDDs function with a read/write head that hovers over rotating platters, which increases the potential for mechanical failure over time. The spinning platters and moving head inside an HDD are both delicate and sensitive to environmental conditions such as vibrations, high temperatures, and even altitude. By contrast, SSDs consist of flash memory technology, wherein information is stored in microchips, thus removing the hazard posed by moving parts.

This ruggedness of SSDs makes them more resistant to shock and vibration, enhancing their lifespan considerably. They can resist damage from accidental drops or system knocks, a quality especially desirable in mobile devices such as laptops and tablets, which are regularly jostled or transported. The non-volatile memory in SSDs also ensures that data isn't lost in the event of sudden power outages.

5.2.1. Longevity through Wear Leveling

To further enhance durability, SSDs employ a technique known as wear leveling. In HDDs, certain sectors tend to be used more frequently, leading to uneven wear and a higher probability of certain sectors failing before others. SSDs counteract this by evenly distributing wear across all the blocks in the device, thereby extending the overall operational lifespan of the drive.

To wrap up, SSDs, with their staggering speeds and robust durability, have certainly staked their claim in the data storage market. They offer significant advantages over HDDs in terms of enhancing both the performance and lifespan of computing systems while also offering benefits in various settings, from everyday computing to data-intensive professional environments. Although SSDs currently come at a higher price point than HDDs, the immense benefits they offer cannot be understated. The further reduction in prices anticipated in the coming years will likely see SSDs dominate the storage market, making them the de facto storage choice for a wide array of devices.

Chapter 6. Understanding SSD Sizes and Interfaces

When delving into the realm of Solid State Drives (SSD), a critical consideration involves understanding their physical sizes and interfaces. SSDs come in a variety of dimensions and can interface with your computer in a myriad of ways - facts which heavily influence their compatibility, performance, and the overall user experience.

To begin such an exhaustive journey examining SSDs, let's start with the physical sizes.

6.1. SSD Physical Sizes

Solid State Drives, also known as flash drives, commingle different form factors setting them apart. Each form factor is designed for specific types of computing devices, from desktops and laptops to enterprise server arrays. Knowing these specifications facilitates selecting an SSD that fits your device perfectly.

The most common SSD form factors that you'll encounter include:

- 2.5-inch: This is the most widespread SSD size, directly replacing traditional Serial ATA (SATA) HDDs. They are typically used in desktop machines and standard laptops.

- M.2: A more recent innovation, these are stick-shaped SSDs chiefly found in ultrabooks, due to their lightweight and minimalistic design.

- mSATA: M.2's predecessor, this can often be found in older ultrabook models.

- PCIe Add-In Card (AIC): This type leads directly into a motherboard's PCIe slot rather than occupying a regular drive bay, using the PCIe lane's high speed function.

Each of these sizes relates not only to the physical dimensions of the SSD but often confines the types of interfaces the drive can use, leading us to our next topic.

6.2. SSD Interfaces and Protocols

An interface plays a significant role in how an SSD connects to and communicates with a computing device. While sizes are about physical compatibility, interfaces and protocols concern technical compatibility and performance. Chief among these interfaces are SATA, PCIe, and NVMe, while AHCI and NVMe stand out as primary storage protocols.

The distinction between an interface and a protocol might seem unclear, so let's iron it out. An interface is a physical connector and its electrical characteristics, whereas a protocol is a set of rules that governs data transfer between components.

1. SATA: This interface has been the universal standard for HDDs and has been adopted for SSDs. SATA-based SSDs generally operate at a maximum speed of 600MB/s, limited by the SATA III standard's maximum throughput.

2. PCIe: A high-speed serial computer expansion bus standard, PCI Express (PCIe) SSDs are faster than SATA SSDs, primarily because of their interface's higher available bandwidth.

3. NVMe: Non-Volatile Memory Express (NVMe) is a protocol designed specifically for flash storage technology. It exploits the capabilities of PCIe, bringing significantly faster data transfer rates.

Now, let's look at the protocols:

• AHCI: Advanced Host Controller Interface (AHCI) is essentially a legacy protocol supports SATA devices. Designed during the era of spinning disks, it doesn't fully exploit SSDs' potential.

- NVMe: As an interface, NVMe drives excel due to the streamlined protocol designed explicitly for SSDs. NVMe boasts reduced latency and increased Input/Output operations Per Second (IOPS) compared to AHCI.

With the basics of physical sizes and interfaces under our belts, we ascend into higher complexity as we delve into intricacies of these interfaces and examine future trends and technologies.

6.3. The Intricacies of Interfaces

Understanding the subtleties of these interfaces requires us to look into how they connect and communicate within a system.

SATA SSDs mirror their hard drive counterparts in terms of appearance and are simple plug-and-play devices, making them favorable for the average consumer. However, their speed cap of 600MB/s renders them far slower than PCIe-based SSDs.

PCIe SSDs, by contrast, leverage the PCIe bus for connections, typically found in M.2 and AIC form factors. While they offer excellent performance, compatibility can be trickier, as not all systems have available PCIe slots, or the BIOS may not support booting from PCIe.

NVMe SSDs stand distinct from SATA and PCIe drives, marked by a dramatic difference in performance. Specifically designed human-computer interfaces improve NVMe drive efficiency by reducing the amount of CPU intervention during data transfer.

6.4. Future Trends and Technologies

Speed, efficiency, and capacity are the driving force behind SSD development. This forward momentum propels the evolution towards more compact sizes and innovative interfaces, with SSD technology continually surpassing its predecessors.

In terms of interfaces, NVMe looks set to dominate the future of SSDs, thanks to its designed-for-SSDs protocol that maximizes flash storage's potential. The advent of NVMe over Fabrics (NVMe-oF), an extension of NVMe allowing it to work over network fabrics, offers even more flexibility and accessibility to storage solutions.

Regarding form factors, the trend toward miniaturization persists, with M.2 being a prominent player due to its size. For businesses and data centers, however, larger form factors like U.2 drives that can deploy high-capacity 2.5-inch SSDs demonstrate more relevance.

Finally, with newly emerging technologies like 3D NAND and Quad-Level Cell (QLC) NAND, SSDs capacity can soar while keeping costs down. These advancements guarantee the burgeoning role SSDs will play in our increasingly data-driven world.

The world of SSD sizes and interfaces might seem complex, but once you break it down, it's merely another component of the beautiful tapestry of technology. As consumer and commercial demands evolve, so too will the technology we use to meet them, moving us tantalizingly forward towards a thrilling future of data storage.

Chapter 7. Data Recovery in SSDs: An Overview

As you delve into the world of Solid State Drives (SSDs), one aspect that inevitably surfaces in your enquiry, is the topic of data recovery. SSDs, despite providing speedier access to data, longer battery life, and more robust endurance to physical damage, present their unique set of challenges when it comes to data recovery.

Understanding why data recovery is a crucial area of discussion when it comes to SSDs requires taking a closer look at how these storage devices operate.

7.1. SSDs and Data Storage Aesthetics

Unlike traditional hard drives, which leveraged a disk-and-needle system to store and read data, SSDs use NAND flash memory. Each piece of data is stored in a cell, and these cells are then grouped into pages. The pages are organized into blocks.

Unlike a hard drive, in which data could be over-written directly on-the-fly, SSDs require a two-step process to overwrite data: erasure, then re-writing. This need for erasure before overwriting is an essential facet of how SSD storage functions and forms the underpinning of data recovery in SSDs.

7.2. The Concept of SSD Endurance

To comprehend the implications of the overwrite protocol in SSD, it is also necessary to understand SSD endurance. Every cell in an SSD has a finite number of times it can be written and erased, also known as its write cycle or endurance.

As SSDs continue to utilize and reuse these cells, the durability of each cell gradually diminishes, and ultimately, they become unable to reliably store data. This degradation is monitored using SMART (Self-Monitoring, Analysis, and Reporting Technology) tools within the SSD's firmware, which predict the drive's 'End of Life'.

7.3. Key Challenges in SSD Data Recovery

There are several significant challenges one may face when attempting data recovery on an SSD, all stemming from the design and functionality of these drives.

1. **Write Amplification:** Because of the erase-write process, SSDs also endure a phenomenon known as write amplification, where the amount of actual physical data written tends to be multiple times the logical amount of data intended to be written.

2. **TRIM command:** This is a command that the OS sends to the SSD when a file is deleted. Its function is to speed up subsequent writes to the drive, but it does so by erasing blocks that store deleted files, making data recovery more difficult.

3. **Data Encryption:** Almost all SSDs use some standard of encryption. And since the encryption keys are held in the SSD controller, not the NAND chips, if the controller fails, data recovery can become almost impossible.

4. **Over-Provisioning:** SSDs often have additional storage capacity beyond what's labelled, which is used in the wear-leveling process. But when data moves into these areas, recovery becomes complex.

5. **Bad Blocks Management:** When the SSD's firmware detects a block that is reaching its write limit or has too many errors, it will replace that block with a spare from its over-provisioning pool and will stop mapping data to that bad block, making data

recovery a hurdle.

7.4. Approaches to SSD Data Recovery

Despite these challenges, SSD data recovery is not an impossibility. Several steps must be followed to increase the chances of successful data recovery. Firstly, one must avoid rewriting data on the drive, use data recovery software, and if all else fails, consider employing the services of a data recovery professional. However, it is crucial to bear in mind that due to the very nature of SSD technology, some data may simply be unrecoverable.

7.5. Future of SSD and Data Recovery

While the path of SSD data recovery may seem fraught with difficulty, new technological advancements are on the horizon to mitigate these issues. Software is being continually updated to handle SSD architecture specifically, and the newer generations of SSDs are being developed to deal better with the limits of NAND technology.

Remember, data loss prevention is always more reliable than data recovery attempts. Regular backup, correct use, and careful monitoring of the SSD's health can go a long way in ensuring our data's longevity and integrity.

The industry continues to evolve, and as we ride this forward wave, we can expect to see the topic of SSD data recovery become less daunting, more manageable, and indeed a fitting puzzle piece in the expanding landscape of SSD technology.

Chapter 8. The Role of SSDs in Enhancing Gaming Experience

Today's high-octane, visually stunning video games require hardware to match. Gone are the days of low-resolution 8-bit graphics and subpar sound. Modern gamers demand titles with immersive worlds, high-res textures, and smooth character animations. One of the key factors influencing this smooth, uninterrupted gaming experience is the Solid-State Drive (SSD).

8.1. The Evolution of Game Storage

Originally, game consoles and personal computers used cartridges or discs as the primary storage medium for games. Even as games started to install directly onto the system's main hard drive, the spinning-disc hard drive (HDD) was the storage of choice. However, as game sizes expanded, the limitations of the HDD began to show. Slower load times, frame rate inconsistencies, and limited lifespan were just a few of these constraints.

The SSD with its quicker read/write speeds and longer lifespan emerged as the solution to these issues. SSDs use flash memory to store data, which allows for faster retrieval and storage. This speed translates directly into a smoother gaming experience, with less waiting and more playing.

8.2. SSDs and Load Times

Ask any avid gamer and they'll tell you – one of the biggest game experience interrupters are slow load times, especially while booting up or during scene transitions. An SSD makes a considerable difference here. With their rapid read speeds, SSDs reduce these load times significantly, allowing you to plunge back into action swiftly.

For example, in a game like "The Elder Scrolls V: Skyrim," which is loaded with large, open-world maps, fast travel points and numerous non-playable characters (NPCs), the benefits of an SSD are evident. Faster load times mean less waiting during fast travel or when entering a new area, leading to a much smoother gaming experience.

8.3. Improving Game Performance

An often-overlooked advantage of SSDs is how they help stabilize game performance. Most modern games are built on complex engines that constantly load and unload data. When a game struggles to fetch data rapidly enough from the hard drive, there might be performance issues, such as dropped frames or stuttering.

On an SSD, data read is much faster, which assists in keeping game performance stable. Textures pop up more quickly, the game engine doesn't struggle as hard, and you'll notice fewer instances of your game stuttering or freezing.

8.4. Reducing Wear and Tear

Gaming involves a lot of data being written and read constantly, which can wear out mechanical drives fairly quickly. SSDs, lacking any physical movement, suffer less wear and tear compared to traditional HDDs. They're robust, durable, and resilient – built to last much longer.

8.5. The Future of SSDs in Gaming

With technology evolving at a rapid pace, the SSD is set to play an even more integral role in gaming. Next-gen gaming consoles like

PlayStation 5 and Xbox Series X have already announced the use of SSDs as their standard storage, heralding a new era for gaming.

These SSDs are not only faster than anything we've seen in consoles so far, but they also let developers create games without being constrained by load times or data streaming speeds. It's reminiscent of the shift from cartridges to discs, where developers found new freedom in the space provided.

8.6. Choosing an SSD for your Gaming

When choosing an SSD, it's essential to consider factors such as storage capacity, speed, and price. Currently, 500GB to 1TB drives are the sweet spot as they provide ample room for multiple games and are reasonably priced. However, with game installations getting larger, investing in a larger capacity SSD, although more expensive, may be beneficial in the long run.

Also, there are two major kinds of SSDs: SATA and NVMe. SATA SSDs are cheaper and slightly slower, while NVMe SSDs are faster and slightly more expensive. For most gamers, a SATA SSD will be more than enough, but if you want the maximum performance possible, an NVMe SSD is the one to choose.

In summary, SSDs provide gamers with a new level of immersion, reduced load times, improved game performance, and reduced wear and tear. As the future of gaming continues to evolve, it's clear that SSDs will play a key role in shaping that future. Despite being slightly more expensive than traditional HDDs, the improvements in gaming experience and durability make SSDs a worthy investment for any serious gamer. And with developments in SSD technology, prices are expected to come down, making it accessible to even more gamers. As such, Solid-State Drives' role in enhancing the gaming experience is only set to grow bigger and more impactful.

Chapter 9. Enterprise Applications of Solid State Drives

Solid state drives (SSDs) are finding their place across various domains in the industry, especially for enterprise applications. SSDs bring in a range of benefits such as faster data access, durability, and lower power consumption, which make them an ideal choice for use in enterprise settings that demand both performance and reliability.

9.1. Understanding Enterprise Applications

Enterprise application comprises software designed to meet the unique needs and objectives of the organizations like businesses, schools, charities, and government organizations. These are powerful, scalable, and complex tools that integrate or encompass several functions like planning, executing, controlling, and administration of the team and individual activities within the organizations.

To help us understand the implications of SSDs for enterprise applications, let's discuss the key areas where SSDs are increasingly embraced.

9.2. Data Centers

Data centers, the heart of an enterprise, are gradually transitioning from Hard Disk Drives (HDDs) to Solid State Drives. HDDs contain mechanically spinning disks with a read/write head on an arm, whereas SSDs use flash memory to deliver superior performance and durability. Given the high input/output operations per second (IOPS) that many enterprises need for their big data analytics and high-performance computing, SSDs offer the advantage of fast and consistent response times.

Moreover, SSD's lack of moving parts results in fewer failures and reduced maintenance costs over time. This is a crucial consideration for data center operations where reliability and uptime are critical. The SSD's need for less physical space and reduced cooling requirements are further triggers for their adoption.

In summary, the switch to SSDs provides data centers a number of advantages including increased storage density, lower total cost of ownership (TCO), boosted performance and speed, reduced power consumption, and improved reliability.

9.3. Cloud Storage

In the age of digital transformation, most enterprises are leveraging cloud storage to store, manage, and process the data. Traditional storage solutions can't always provide the speed required for these cloud applications to perform optimally. Here's where SSDs come into play. With their ability to provide high-speed data processing and scalable storage, they contribute to fluid, real-time operations on the cloud.

Moreover, due to lower latency, data from an SSD hosted cloud can be accessed faster, improving application performance, which is crucial for real-time processing needs of many mission-critical applications.

9.4. Server Storage

Faster read/write speeds make SSDs an ideal choice for server-side applications. Popular enterprise software applications, such as

Database Management Systems (DBMS) or Customer Relationship Management (CRM) systems, often require swift data access for efficient operation. SSDs can facilitate this faster access, thereby improving overall server efficiency and application performance.

9.5. Virtual Desktop Infrastructure (VDI)

The virtual desktop infrastructure is another domain where SSDs are proving beneficial. In a VDI environment, maintaining performance during peak demand is critical. SSDs, with their benefits of faster data access and lower latency, provide a substantial performance boost during these peak loads. Given their reliability and endurance, SSDs help ensure a consistent and high-performing desktop experience for users.

9.6. Video Surveillance Systems

SSDs are ideal for video surveillance systems, as these systems require high write endurance and storage capabilities to handle continuous recording and playbacks. Additionally, the superior speed of SSDs allows faster data retrieval and real-time monitoring.

Financial constraints, which previously reduced the adoption of SSDs, have lessened due to the decrease in the cost-per-gigabyte over the years. Thus, allowing a more widespread utility of SSDs across diverse enterprise applications.

9.7. Conclusion

The advantages offered by SSDs including high-speed, reliability, lower cooling requirements, and reduced need for physical space make them an ideal choice for enterprise applications. Adoption of SSDs in the enterprise space is set to grow significantly over the next few years, influenced by the continued decline in SSD prices and demand for high-performing, reliable, and scalable data storage solutions. As enterprises continue to move towards more digital and real-time operations, the role of SSDs in everything from data centers to cloud storage and server storage will continue to expand.

The full gamut of benefits associated with SSD integration clearly validates the business rationale behind the seismic shift from traditional forms of storage to SSDs for enterprise applications.

Chapter 10. Exploring Types of SSDs: SLC, MLC, TLC, and QLC

Within the realm of solid-state drives (SSDs), diversification reflects the myriad storage requirements of modern technology users. The inherent suitability of SSDs for specific tasks and applications predominantly depends on the cell structure they adopt. Their cell structures are categorized into Single-Level Cell (SLC), Multi-Level Cell (MLC), Triple-Level Cell (TLC), and Quad-Level Cell (QLC).

10.1. Single-Level Cell (SLC)

SLCs represent the very pinnacle of SSD technology in terms of performance, longevity, and reliability. Here's a detailed explanation:

Single-Level Cells store a single bit of information in each physical cell. This simple mechanism minimizes the chance for errors, as there are only two possible states: "0" or "1". The minimalistic approach translates to faster write times and longer lifespan compared to other SSDs. However, this premium performance comes with a hefty price tag, making SLC SSDs typically found in high-demand commercial and enterprise environments that prioritize data integrity and durability over cost factors.

Advantages	Disadvantages	Class-best durability (Approx. 100,000 write cycles)

| Highest Cost per Cell | Rapid write capability | Less storage capacity for a given size |

10.2. Multi-Level Cell (MLC)

The MLC SSDs strike a balance between cost and performance. Here's the in-depth rundown:

Multi-Level Cells can store two bits of information per cell. This doubling of data capacity in each cell reduces costs per GB significantly when compared to SLC SSDs. However, there's a trade-off. More information per cell implies a higher probability of error, which can affect the SSD's performance and decrease its lifespan. Advanced error correction algorithms and firmware are employed to mitigate this focus on potential errors and data loss.

Advantages	Disadvantages	More Cost-Effective compared to SLC SSDs
Reduced Longevity (Approx. 10,000 write cycles)	Decent performance	Slower write speeds compared to SLC SSDs

10.3. Triple-Level Cell (TLC)

TLC models are the most common type of SSDs found in consumer devices. Here's why:

Triple-Level Cells store three bits of data per cell. This increase in data capacity per cell makes TLC SSDs incredibly cost-effective, making them regularly found in consumer laptops, desktops, and some business applications. Still, the additional bit means even slower write times and shorter lifespan than MLCs. Manufacturers often offset slowdown by a cache system where data is written as if it's MLC or SLC, before being erased and rewritten as TLC when the drive is less active.

Advantages	Disadvantages	Predominately cost-effective
Shorter lifespan (Approx. 1,000 to 3,000 write cycles)	Adequate for most consumer needs	Slower write speeds than MLC SSDs

10.4. Quad-Level Cell (QLC)

QLCs are a recent addition to the SSD landscape, alluring by their high storage capacity at a lower cost. Here's the detailed narrative:

Quad-Level Cells store an impressive four bits of data per cell. This expanded capacity significantly reduces the cost per GB, making QLC SSDs ideal for users prioritizing storage volume over speed and durability. However, achieving this high storage density means that QLC SSDs have the slowest write speeds among the types and the shortest lifespan. They are more suited for applications with significant data storage requirements but don't frequently write data.

Advantages	Disadvantages	Optimal cost per GB
Shortest lifespan (Approx. 100 to 1,000 write cycles)	Substantial storage density	Slowest write speeds among SSDs

While the cost-per-GB advantage offered by TLC and QLC drives is alluring, it's imperative to consider their lifespan and performance tradeoffs. Whether it's enterprise-grade SLCs or large storage QLCs, understanding these four types can help pinpoint the right SSD for any given application. If reliability is a priority, SLCs and MLCs stand out. If cost or high capacity is the focus, you might veer towards TLC or QLC. In a nutshell, remember – the right SSD type, like all technology, comes down to choosing based on specific needs and priorities.

Chapter 11. The Promising Future: Innovations and Trends in SSD Technology

The rapid evolution of Solid State Drive (SSD) technology is inspiring a new wave of innovation within the field of data storage. SSDs, renowned for their lightning-fast performance, durability, and efficiency, are shaping the future of high-tech industries, from artificial intelligence and machine learning to cloud computing and the Internet of Things (IoT).

11.1. SSDs and AI: A Formidable Partnership

In the realm of Artificial Intelligence (AI) and Machine Learning (ML), SSDs are transformative. AI and ML require significant amounts of data to function effectively, with applications often running thousands, if not millions, of computations per second. These applications require instant data access, and SSDs, with their faster data retrieval times, are up to the task.

The future forecasts SSDs with even higher capacities and faster input/output access speeds. This potential technological leap bodes well for AI-based applications, allowing them to manage larger datasets and operate even more efficiently. Moreover, the expected advancements in SSD technology could further empower AI-driven predictive analysis, potentially saving businesses millions of dollars and significantly enhancing our daily life.

11.2. Changing The Game: SSDs And Cloud Computing

As more businesses move to cloud-based storage solutions, the demands for more efficient and reliable storage technologies are escalating. SSDs are charting an innovative path in cloud computing as they offer superior performance in comparison to traditional HDDs.

The herald of high-performing SSDs enables cloud storage providers to offer quicker data access and transfer rates, improving the functionality and user experience of cloud services. Ongoing research in SSD technology is likely to result in increased storage capacities and improved data access speeds, making SSDs even more viable for cloud storage.

In the near future, SSDs are expected to dominate the cloud computing landscape, paving the way for greater storage efficiency, faster retrieval times, and overall improved performance.

11.3. The IoT Revolution And SSDs

The IoT is an evolving field with millions of interconnected devices constantly generating and transmitting data. Such an environment necessitates quick, reliable, and durable data storage solutions.

The fact that they are less likely to fail under strenuous conditions makes SSDs a perfect fit for IoT devices, particularly those installed in extreme environments such as industrial settings or outdoor locations. As the IoT continues to grow, we expect that the demand for SSDs will increase instrumentally, presenting an overwhelming opportunity for advancements in SSD technology.

As IoT devices generate enormous amounts of data daily, future SSDs may feature even more considerable storage capacities and enhanced durability features to withstand the demands of IoT deployments.

11.4. Environmental Considerations and SSDs

While SSD technology evolves for escalating demands, designers are tirelessly working to minimize their environmental footprint. New-generation SSDs are being designed to consume less power without compromising performance. The consequences of this approach are twofold: lower electricity usage reduces the environmental impact, and simultaneously, it reduces the cooling requirements for data centers, generating further power savings.

Future SSD developments are also likely to address e-waste concerns. As old storage devices become obsolete, proper recycling is a growing concern. Future SSDs may be designed for easy disassembly and recycling, minimizing electronic waste and environmental damage. Could we eventually see biodegradable SSDs? It's not out of the question.

11.5. The Future: More Than Just Storage

The future of SSD technology extends well beyond just improved storage capacities. Advancements may include the ability to process data directly on the drive itself, a technology often referred to as computational storage. This will reduce the need for data to move between the processor and storage, vastly increasing overall system efficiency and speed.

Likewise, advances in controller technology will further enhance SSD performance, increasing the speed at which data is accessed or written while ensuring data integrity and reliability.

In conclusion, the promising future of SSD technology is not just about escalating data capacity or faster access times, but encapsulates a more extensive range of factors including environmental considerations, integration with AI, Cloud and IoT, and even advanced features such as computational storage. The quick-paced evolution of SSD technology is setting the stage for a radical transformation in the way we store, access, and process data in the future.

www.ingramcontent.com/pod-product-compliance
Lightning Source LLC
LaVergne TN
LVHW051634050326
832903LV00033B/4754